BASEBALL HALL OF FAMERS

Nolan Ryan

Ellyn Sanna

the rosen publishing group's
rosen
central

Published in 2003 by The Rosen Publishing Group, Inc.
29 East 21st Street, New York, NY 10010

Library of Congress Cataloging-in-Publication Data

Sanna, Ellyn, 1958–
Nolan Ryan / by Ellyn Sanna.— 1st ed.
   p. cm. — (Baseball Hall of Famers)
Summary: Looks at the life and career of Nolan Ryan, who overcame personal and professional challenges to become one of baseball's most powerful pitchers.
Includes bibliographical references (p.) and index.
ISBN 0-8239-3601-5
1. Ryan, Nolan, 1947– —Juvenile literature. 2. Baseball players—United States—Biography—Juvenile literature.
[1. Ryan, Nolan, 1947– 2. Baseball players.]
I. Title. II. Series.
GV865.R9 S36 2003
796.357'092—dc21

                                        2002002421

Manufactured in the United States of America

Contents

Legendary pitcher Nolan Ryan, seen here in 1983, compiled 53 major-league baseball records during his twenty-seven-season career. He threw an unsurpassed 5,714 strikeouts and 7 no-hitters. He also won 324 games.

Introduction

L ike any other small-town kid, Nolan Ryan enjoyed riding his bike and swimming with his friends. Young Nolan loved animals, and he hated school. He struggled to learn how to read and he needed help to learn how to speak clearly. But the thing that made him different from most kids his age was his fastball.

When Nolan was still in high school, his pitching attracted the attention of a scout from the New York Mets. At the time, Nolan was dreaming of being a veterinarian or a rancher or maybe a basketball player, but that scout saw Nolan's potential for greatness at something else—baseball.

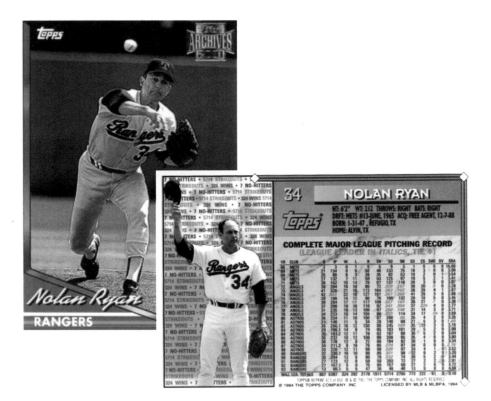

Shown here are some of Nolan Ryan's baseball cards, which are traded by fans around the country. Ryan's rookie card, which also features another rookie, Jerry Koosman, is valued in mint condition at a whopping $1,600.

Nolan more than lived up to the scout's expectations. In Nolan Ryan's twenty-seven-season career, he broke record after record. His fastball was so fast that he struck out even the greatest players of all, stars like Hank Aaron, Roberto Clemente, Mark McGwire, and Sammy Sosa. Year after year, long after most players would have retired, Nolan kept pitching—until finally he had struck out more batters than any other pitcher before him. Scientists once measured his pitch at faster than 100 miles per hour, so it was no wonder he earned the record for the most no-hit games, or no-hitters. His pitches were just too fast to hit!

Despite his powerful pitch, his baseball years were not always easy. He had plenty of personal and professional challenges to overcome on the road to success. But in 1999, when Nolan Ryan took his place in Cooperstown's Baseball Hall of Fame, he had certainly earned his right to be there. He is truly one of baseball's brightest stars.

Nolan Ryan gives a speech during his induction into the Baseball Hall of Fame in 1999. Ryan's 2,416 strikeouts with the Angels alone would rank in baseball's career top thirty, just ahead of Sandy Koufax's 2,396 lifetime outs.

Baseball's
Highest Honor

O n July 25, 1999, Nolan Ryan woke up very early. A big day lay ahead. He, his wife, and his children had spent the night in the Otesaga Resort in Cooperstown, New York.

Cooperstown is a small town, home to only 2,500 people. It lies at the tip of Otsego Lake, one of the Finger Lakes in upstate New York.

Every hotel was full that day. But Nolan Ryan hadn't had to worry about finding a room. He was guest of honor at Cooperstown's Baseball Hall of Fame.

Cooperstown is much more than a sleepy little town surrounded by rolling farmland.

It's a town that celebrates excellence in baseball. Nolan Ryan was about to be inducted into Cooperstown's Baseball Hall of Fame, the highest honor a baseball player can receive.

To win this honor, a player needs to have played more than a few good games. Playing an amazing season isn't enough, either. Instead, a player needs to have played excellently for an entire career. His record needs to contain at least 3,000 hits, 500 homers, or 300 wins. Baseball writers hold elections every year to vote on which players deserve to be admitted into the Hall of Fame. Their standards are high.

The standards were set when the Hall of Fame opened in 1939 by the five baseball legends who were its first members: Ty Cobb, Walter Johnson, Christy Mathewson, Babe Ruth, and Honus Wagner, all shining examples of baseball excellence. Cobb smashed 4,191 hits in the twenty-four seasons he played. During his twenty-one-year career, Johnson's sidearm fastball helped him strike out 3,508 batters, winning 416 games. Mathewson's fadeaway

The Baseball Hall of Fame's Class of 1999 *(left to right)*: Orlando Cepeda, Robin Yount, Nolan Ryan, and George Brett

pitch was pretty amazing, too. It helped him win 373 games in his seventeen seasons. Babe Ruth whacked 714 homers during his twenty-two-season career; and Wagner played seventeen straight seasons with a batting average over .300. These five spectacular players were elected to the Hall of Fame in 1936, before it even opened. By the time the hall opened, three years later, twenty more players had been added to the list, including Cy Young, Lou

Gehrig, and Grover Cleveland Alexander. By 1999, the membership had climbed from 25 to 201 men. Each player was one of baseball's very best. And now Nolan Ryan would join these shining ranks.

Nolan had more than earned his place during his twenty-seven-year career. He had won 324 games and struck out 5,714 batters. He had pitched 7 no-hitters and 12 one-hitters. Nolan played six seasons in which he had gotten over 300 strikeouts. Once, he had struck out 383 batters in a single season.

Nolan Ryan's numbers were truly amazing. One of his pitches had been clocked at more than 100 miles an hour! No one had ever thrown a faster ball than Nolan. That pitch made *The Guinness Book of World Records*. The umpire who saw it said the ball seemed to "explode" when it got to the plate.

Most batters weren't quick enough for Nolan's fastball. He had struck out ace hitter Mark McGwire three times in one game. In fact, Nolan struck out all the great hitters of his time, from Hank Aaron to Sammy Sosa.

Nolan's pitch was just too fast! A hitter facing his fastball had less than half a second to react. Even slugger Reggie Jackson struck out twenty-two times against Nolan. Reggie is reported to have said, "Nolan Ryan was the only pitcher I was ever scared to face."

Fastball pitchers usually have short careers because of the stress on their arms. But Nolan defied the odds. In his forties, he was a better pitcher than he had been in his twenties. He just seemed to keep getting better. Over and over, he broke baseball records. He set fifty-three major-league records for pitching. This astonishing record was what took Nolan Ryan to Cooperstown that July morning in 1999.

He and his family began the day by attending a sumptuous brunch held by the Texas Rangers on the grounds of the Fenimore Museum. The brunch was attended by the Rangers' current owner, Tom Hicks. Also present was their former owner, George W. Bush, who would later go on to become the president of the United States. About 150 of Nolan Ryan's friends and family were also present, including

Then Texas governor George W. Bush shares a laugh with Nolan Ryan on the eve of Ryan's induction into the Baseball Hall of Fame. Bush owned the Texas Rangers when Ryan was a starting pitcher with the team.

his brother and four sisters. This was a time for everyone who knew Nolan Ryan to celebrate his achievements in baseball.

But Nolan probably didn't have long to chat with his friends, family, and acquaintances. Soon he was rushed off to the day's main event—the induction ceremony.

By then, about 50,000 fans were crowding Cooperstown. The Hall of Fame is on Main

Street, but the crowd couldn't fit inside the building so the ceremony was held at the Clark Sports Center, outside town. Millions were watching the event on a live ESPN broadcast.

As the ceremony began, thirty-four baseball legends came on stage, including Hank Aaron, Reggie Jackson, Willie Mays, Stan Musial, Tom Seaver, and Ted Williams. These were baseball's living legends, men who were already members of the Hall of Fame. As they filed into place, they left the front row empty for the four newest stars—Nolan Ryan, Orlando Cepeda, George Brett, and Robin Yount. Brett's twenty-one-season career with the Kansas City Royals had included 3,154 hits. In 1966, Cepeda became the first unanimous MVP in the National League since Carl Hubbell in 1936. Robin Yount had accumulated 3,142 hits in his twenty seasons with the Milwaukee Brewers.

Nolan and the other players took their places, and the ceremony began. When it was Nolan's turn to be honored, he walked across the stage. Baseball commissioner Bud Selig unveiled a shiny plaque and read from it, "A fierce competitor . . . overwhelming fastball." He went on to read the numbers that told Nolan's story of excellence, and then it was Nolan's turn to speak.

Nolan acknowledged his wife and family, and then he spoke a few words to recognize the contributions of his junior high and high school coaches. Then he thanked the many people who had helped him with his accomplishments. Last of all, he thanked his fans. "I was truly blessed by the fans," he said. "I may be gone, but I won't forget you. And I appreciate all those times that you supported me over the twenty-seven years.

"My ability to throw a baseball was a gift," he told the crowd of 50,000 gathered there. "It was a God-given gift. I had the pleasure . . . to live a childhood dream . . ."

A Boy from
the Country

Lynn Nolan Ryan Jr. was born on January 31, 1947, the youngest of six children, in Refugio, Texas. His family called him Nolan because his father's name was also Lynn. His father's family had lived in Texas for more than a hundred years, but they had originally come from Ireland. His mother, Martha Lee Hancock, was thought to be related to John Hancock, the famous signer of the Declaration of Independence.

Nolan's father worked as a supervisor for an oil company called Pan American. When Nolan was about six months old, the company asked his father to work at an oil refinery near Houston. The family settled in Alvin, Texas, a small, quiet country village, with a population of about 5,000, just twenty miles south of Houston. Nolan's mother liked the small-town atmosphere, the tree-lined streets, and the good schools for her children.

Nolan's father worked long hours, but he was home every evening and weekend. While he was working, Nolan's mother ran the household. As the youngest child, Nolan also had five siblings to look after him: four big sisters—Lynda, Mary Lou, Judy, and Jean—and a big brother—Robert. Robert was seven years older than Nolan, but once Nolan was old enough, Robert let him tag along while he played ball with his friends. He taught Nolan to play catch in their backyard, and they turned a vacant lot into a baseball field. Nolan and the other children spent hours on that field.

Since the town was close to the Gulf of Mexico, the air was always hot and humid and full of mosquitoes. Sometimes Nolan and his friends would head out for the swampy bayou, where they would throw stones. They would usually spot a target and cheer if the stones hit their mark.

Nolan loved to throw almost anything at any target. "I was throwing something or other all the time," he said later. "My mother was constantly on me about breaking windows."

Nolan's father decided to encourage him to find a better use for his arm—baseball. When Nolan was seven, his father took him to the sporting goods section of the Alvin hardware store.

Nolan was excited. As the youngest of six, he seldom had anything new just for himself. Most of his possessions were hand-me-downs, already well worn. The Ryans weren't poor, but with such a large family, they seldom had enough money left over for extras. But Nolan's father must have understood what his son needed. He helped him pick out a brand new Nocona glove.

That glove became Nolan's most treasured possession. At first, he even slept with it at night. And when he grew up, he still kept it.

When Nolan was nine, he joined Little League baseball. Within a couple of years he had pitched his first no-hitter. Nolan had

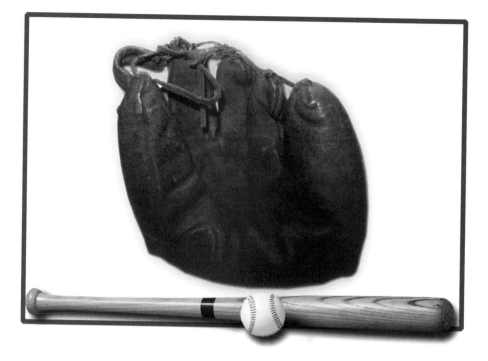

This is the actual baseball glove that Nolan Ryan's father gave him when the future hall-of-famer was just seven years old.

played just about every position he could, and he had made the all-star team. "I was successful," Nolan said, looking back as an adult, "but not superior to the other kids. I could always throw farther than the other kids—not harder, just farther."

Nolan was proud of his Little League uniform. He and his friends wore their baseball caps everywhere, even to school. His team was called the Rangers, after the Texas law enforcement agency. No one could have guessed that nearly forty years later, Nolan would play for another Texan team called the Rangers!

As a child, Nolan listened to a speech at a Little League awards ceremony and thought for the first time about being a major league baseball player. The speaker talked about how some day one of the Little Leaguers might go on to play in the major leagues. Nolan must have felt as though a bell had gone off in his head as excitement surged through him. Years later, he would still remember that moment: the hot sun, the field, the speaker's words. Although he had no way of knowing the direction his life would take, the memory stuck with him.

Nolan had seen his first major league baseball game a few years earlier, but not in person. Instead, on Saturday afternoons, he and his family watched *Game of the Week* on the family's first television set. During the rest of the week, when games were not broadcast on television, fans listened to them on the radio. But Nolan was usually too busy.

He liked to ride around town on his bike with his friends, with baseball cards whirring in his wheel spokes. He and his friends collected and traded the cards, and they also belonged to the Cub Scouts. Growing up, Nolan had a lot of freedom to go where he wanted when he wanted, especially during the summer when there was no school, but he always knew to come home in time for supper.

At dinnertime, the entire Ryan family would gather around the table, and their father would say grace. The family would talk over their day while they ate. Mrs. Ryan made meat, potatoes, and a dessert every night. She was a good cook, and Nolan especially liked his mother's fried chicken. He didn't like the nights when they were expected to eat beets. Beet night was once a week, and the rule was that each child had to eat two beets. Nolan hated beets, but he ate them. If he didn't, he knew he would miss dessert. His favorite was chocolate pie.

On Sundays, the Ryans attended Sunday school and morning worship at the Alvin Methodist Church, where Nolan sang in the youth choir.

Nolan loved animals. His constant companion was Suzy, a white fox terrier. One day Suzy chased a skunk into a pile of brush. Nolan followed. He soon found he had made a big mistake. When he and Suzy came dragging home, accompanied by a foul-smelling cloud of odor, Nolan's mother gave them both a bath in tomato juice to neutralize the skunk odor—but it wasn't much fun for either the boy or the dog!

Another time, while Nolan was going to a field with a metal pan to pick blueberries, a pack of wild dogs threatened to attack Suzy. Suzy was no match for the ferocious dogs, and she stood trembling at Nolan's side. With his lips curled back, the lead dog darted in at her, and Nolan smashed the pan on the dog's muzzle. With a yelp of surprise, the dog fell back. Nolan snatched up Suzy and dashed to safety.

When Nolan was twelve, he bought a two-day-old calf for two dollars and fifty cents. The calf was too young to eat feed, so Nolan fed it from a bottle. When the calf was frightened by a thunderstorm, Nolan brought it into the safety of the garage. He held the calf, feeding it from its bottle, while the storm exploded outside.

When the calf was grown, Nolan sold it and bought two more calves with the profit he made. Eventually, he rented a pasture outside town and continued to earn money by raising calves. His love of ranching and cattle would stay with him as he grew to adulthood.

By the time Nolan was thirteen, Houston had its own major league baseball team—the Colt .45s. When the indoor Astrodome opened six years later, the Colt .45s changed their name to the Houston Astros. In the meantime, the team played outdoors, the fans swatting mosquitoes while they watched. Nolan was in the stands whenever he had the chance.

Nolan Ryan was seven years old when his father bought him his first glove.
Here he is pictured in his Little League uniform.

But most of the time Nolan was too busy for baseball games. Like the others in his family, he was expected to work hard to help earn money for college.

The Ryans worried about how they would be able to afford a college education for their six children. To earn the extra money, Nolan's father took a second job delivering newspapers. Everyone in the family, including Nolan and his brother and sisters, helped with the paper route.

Every day, from the time Nolan was in second grade until he was in high school, along with his father and his brother, Robert, Nolan got up at one in the morning. They drove to an abandoned gas station in Alvin where the papers had been left by the delivery truck. Stacks of the *Houston Post* were waiting for them, piled high. The Ryans rolled the papers and tied them with strings. Nolan developed strong hands from this daily work.

When enough papers were ready, Mr. Ryan and Robert took off to deliver them.

Nolan stayed behind to roll and tie the rest. He could roll a stack of fifty papers in five minutes. By the time his father and brother came back, he had the rest ready for them. Around four or five in the morning, he went home to catch a few more hours of sleep.

Despite the hard work, Nolan enjoyed his childhood years. The only thing he didn't like was school. School was a challenge for Nolan, one that he would have avoided if he possibly could. Unfortunately, he didn't have that choice. A few times he even had to go to summer school.

Nolan was intelligent, but he didn't learn like other children his age. He had struggled with reading and writing. Numbers were hard for him, too. It was hard to understand what he was saying because he had a lisp. Today, Nolan would probably have been eligible for a special program for learning-disabled students, but back in the 1950s, most schools lacked programs for students like Nolan. Instead, his teachers tried to make him repeat grades.

Nolan's mother persuaded the school to let him attend summer school instead, and that's what Nolan did for three summers. While his friends were outside playing, Nolan sat in a hot, sweaty classroom. Nothing really helped, either. He continued to have learning problems.

But none of that mattered when Nolan had a ball in his hand. Sports became the area in which he could succeed. Because he excelled on the playing field, he won the admiration of both his teachers and friends. And Nolan was committed to becoming even better.

High School Days

Nolan's fourteenth birthday was a big event in his life because he was old enough to get a Texas driver's license. Nolan couldn't wait. He started looking for a car and finally settled on a nine-year-old, two-door Chevy sedan. It was fire-engine red, it ran well, and it cost him fifty dollars. Nolan thought it was the perfect car.

Now that Nolan could drive, he could cover the rural part of the family paper route while his father delivered the papers in town. Some people have said that Nolan developed his strong arm by throwing newspapers out the car window while he drove. But Nolan was a right-handed pitcher, and he threw the newspapers with his left hand, keeping his right hand on the steering wheel. The newspaper route did teach him other important skills.

Getting up at one in the morning every day taught Nolan the importance of commitment and hard work. He learned that if you have a goal and stick with it through the hard times, eventually you can accomplish more than you ever dreamed.

Despite the grueling schedule of the paper route, Nolan's high school years were happy. Although he still struggled with his grades, sports were a bigger and bigger part of his life.

During gym class, he was dynamite at dodgeball, which his school called bombardment. Two teams would stand on opposite sides of the gym, with volleyballs lined up along the middle line. When the coach blew his whistle, the players would thunder forward to grab the balls. The players would try to grab a ball and heave it at someone on the opposite team. If the person was hit, he was "out."

The game continued until just one person was left—and that person was often Nolan. Whenever he got the ball, everyone else scrambled for the corners. The other kids hated to be hit by his hard, fast balls.

At this point in his life, Nolan thought he was better at basketball than he was at baseball. His fastball was getting even faster, but his pitches were wild and he didn't have much of a curveball. The coach thought that at least two pitchers on their high school team were better than Nolan.

Meanwhile, Nolan had grown to be six feet, two inches tall, and he could jump high. Playing center for his school's basketball team, he dreamed of some day playing college basketball. "All I thought about in high school was basketball," he said later in his autobiography. He led his team—the Yellowjackets—to 27-4 records two years in a row.

When he was fifteen, Nolan went on his first date. Now his thoughts included Ruth Holdorf as well as basketball. She was two years younger than Nolan. They had first noticed each other back when Ruth came to watch Nolan's Little League games. Now they began to go steady. Since Nolan had a car, he could take her to the movies on Friday nights. Afterward, they got a soda at the Dairyland.

They found they had plenty of things to talk about because they both loved sports. Ruth was as athletic as Nolan. In tenth grade, she won the state high school championship in tennis doubles. She also liked playing baseball and basketball.

Sometimes Nolan, Ruth, and Mr. Ryan drove to Houston to watch a baseball game at Colt Stadium. When the Astrodome opened, Nolan and his friends would drive down to watch the Astros.

Nolan was a big fan of Sandy Koufax, the great left-handed Dodger pitcher. Nolan watched once while Koufax struck out eight batters and won the game. Nolan's other two baseball heroes were legendary outfielders Hank Aaron and Roberto Clemente. Nolan admired their hustle, the way they put their all into their playing.

But as much as Nolan loved to watch baseball games, he always thought that this was the closest he would ever get to the major leagues. All that changed, though, when Nolan met Red Murff.

The Houston Astrodome, home of the Houston Astros. As a child Ryan went there to watch baseball games. Nolan played for the Astros from 1979 to 1988. His three-year, $3.5 million deal was the first million-dollar-a-year contract in baseball history.

Red was a baseball scout for the New York Mets. He traveled around the country looking for the best high school baseball players who he could sign on for the Mets. Red was good at spotting boys with great potential.

One Saturday morning in March 1963, Red had an extra hour to spare as he drove between Galveston and Houston. On a whim, he decided to stop by Alvin High School. By luck, a baseball game was going on. It was early in the game when Red got there, and Alvin High was in trouble. The coach had just put in a new pitcher, a tall, skinny kid. Red watched while the kid threw two fastballs. The batter hit the third pitch, a curveball, and got a double.

Technically, the pitcher hadn't done well. After all, he'd just given up a double. But Red didn't care about the curveball. He was thinking about the two fastballs. They were some of the fastest he'd ever seen. After the game, Red went up to the pitcher, Nolan Ryan, and introduced himself.

That night Red watched a major league game in Houston. He knew that the two pitchers—Jim Maloney of the Cincinnati Reds and Turk Farrell of Houston—both had ninety-five-mile-per-hour fastballs. He also knew that the tenth-grader he had seen pitch earlier that day had thrown faster than either of them. Nolan's fastball was "in the hundred-mile-per-hour range," Red wrote that night in his report to the Mets. Red Murff could hardly contain his excitement.

Major league baseball scout John Robert "Red" Murff, pictured here in his home in Texas, is best known for discovering Nolan Ryan.

Later that year, Red went back to Alvin and talked with Nolan's baseball coach and the high school athletics director. He told them that they had "one of the ten best arms in the world" in their school. He advised them not to put Nolan in a weight program for football or mess with his pitching arm in any way. He told them to just let Nolan throw the baseball. He encouraged Coach Jim Watson, the baseball coach, to have confidence in Nolan and let him practice his fastball.

Watson didn't have a lot of experience with baseball. "We only played baseball because the state made us," he is reported to have said later. But Murff knew that Ryan had a special talent, and he didn't want it damaged. In fact, Murff predicted that Nolan would take Alvin High to the state baseball championships.

From then on, whenever Nolan Ryan pitched, either Red Murff or his assistant was there to watch.

Nolan was amazed by Red's attention, but he wasn't quite convinced by Red's confidence in him. He still thought he was better at basketball than he was at baseball.

In his senior year, Nolan couldn't wait for basketball season to start. The year before he had led his team in eighteen straight wins, but in the end, they had been defeated by their rival, Clear Creek, who won the district title, shutting Alvin out of the play-offs. Nolan had made up his mind that this year things would be different.

Instead, the year went just like the year before. Again the Alvin Yellowjackets won twenty-seven games out of thirty-one. And again, Clear Creek defeated them, keeping them out of the play-offs yet again. Nolan was frustrated. He used his frustration to fuel his energy for the baseball season. Alvin High had never been a baseball champion, but Nolan was determined to see that change. He wasn't going to let his senior year go by without leading his school to glory.

Nolan shared pitching duties with another player, a junior. When he wasn't pitching, Nolan played right field; he also batted cleanup. The reputation of his fastball, however, was what made the other teams fear him. When Nolan pitched, Alvin High usually won.

Red Murff still had his eye on Nolan. Now he wanted his boss, Bing Devine, to see Nolan pitch, too. Red could hardly wait to show off his new-found discovery.

The Alvin team had made it into the district games, where the local high schools played each other. Even with Nolan as their pitcher, though, Alvin High had two 1–0 losses, and Coach Watson was angry and frustrated with his players. At a punishment practice he had all the players run until they threw up. Then he made them take turns batting against Nolan, whom he told to pitch as hard as he could. By the end of the practice, the entire team was exhausted. Nolan's pitching arm was hanging like a limp noodle.

And that was when Coach Watson got the big call from Red Murff. Bing Devine was coming to Alvin High to watch Nolan pitch the next day. Coach Watson tried to explain that Nolan wouldn't be pitching; his arm was spent. Red wouldn't listen. "This is it," he insisted. "This is his one shot to make the major leagues."

The next day Alvin played against Channelview. Only a few spectators attended, but Red Murff and Bing Devine were there in the bleachers. Red was ready to show off the new talent he'd been bragging about for the past three years. Nolan took the mound.

He was terrible. His pitches were either wild or they were hit. By the time Coach Watson replaced him in the third inning, Alvin High was losing 7–0. Nolan had just blown his best shot at the majors. Devine shook his head at Red Murff. Red was free to try to make a case for Nolan to the management, he said, but based on what Devine had seen, he couldn't recommend Nolan as a draft choice.

At that point in his life Nolan wasn't even convinced he wanted to play major league baseball. He didn't let the terrible game destroy his confidence or his determination to bring the Alvin Yellowjackets to triumph. The team went on to win the rest of their games, finishing with a 24-8 record, 8-2 in their district. Then they defeated Deer Park—and they were on their way to the play-offs. The Yellowjackets did just as well there.

While the play-offs were beginning, Nolan's senior year came to an end. Nolan was named Outstanding Athlete at his graduation. About the same time, Red Murff called.

As it turned out, Murff had submitted Ryan's name and Nolan had been drafted by the Mets during the eighth round of the 1965 amateur draft. Ryan was the 295th player picked. Red was the only scout who had believed in Nolan. The others suggested that he play college baseball before he took a shot at the major leagues.

Nolan shrugged off the news. He was still too focused on high school baseball to care what the major leaguers thought about him. Thanks to Nolan's pitching, the Alvin Yellowjackets were headed to Austin for the championship game. Red Murff had been proven right after all.

Nolan Ryan works on his pitching during spring training with the Texas Rangers in 1993. It was with the Rangers, on May 1, 1991, at the age of forty-four, that he pitched his seventh career no-hitter.

In the end, Alvin High finished second in the state, and Nolan Ryan was their star player. He had won five games in the state tournament, pitching a no-hitter and batting .700. Named to the all-star team, Nolan finished up the season with a 20–3 record.

Nolan's dream of excelling in high school baseball had come true. But now he had to turn his attention to the future.

The Big Time

On June 28, 1965, Nolan, his parents, Red Murff, and a local sportswriter sat around the Ryans' kitchen table. In the center of the table lay a contract. The Mets were offering Nolan $20,000 to sign. That seemed like a lot of money. Almost everyone at the table was convinced that Nolan should sign.

Nolan was the only one who was undecided. He knew that there were many players the Mets had picked ahead of him in the amateur draft. With that kind of competition, he didn't think he'd ever make it from the Mets minor league teams to the majors.

He was considering a few other options instead. First, he thought he might like to play baseball in college while he studied to be a veterinarian. After all, he had always loved animals, and he thought he would enjoy working with them full-time. He'd always wanted to be a cattle rancher. Or, he thought, he might quit both school and baseball, and just get a full-time job. He wanted to set up a home with Ruth when she graduated, and he knew he would need an income.

As he considered his options, Nolan must have looked across the table at his father. He might have thought about the years his father had worked so hard to support the family. He could have remembered the early mornings, day after day, when his father had delivered newspapers before going to work at the oil refinery—all so the Ryan children would one day be able to go to college.

Suddenly, the sports reporter broke the silence. "What's the matter with you, boy?" he shouted. "You crazy? That man is offering you a sizable amount of money to go and play a game! I'd sign if I were you."

Nolan signed.

After that, Nolan didn't have time to look back. He was to report immediately to a rookie league, the Mets' Marion, Virginia, team in the Appalachian League.

A few days later, he was at the Houston airport, saying good-bye to Ruth and his mother. This would be his first time on an airplane, and his first time away from home. He got lost on his way to Marion, and although he finally ended up in the right place, he couldn't help but wonder if he had done the right thing.

His doubts grew in the weeks that followed. He didn't even have a uniform at first, and when he finally got one, it was too short.

Rookie league baseball was very different from high school baseball. The team spent much of their time on long bus rides. When they played, it was on bad fields with dim lights and small locker rooms. One by one, players were cut from the team and sent back home. Nolan was scared, homesick, and lonely. He missed Ruth.

The best thing that happened that summer was that Ruth's father drove her up to Virginia for a visit. The rest of the time, Nolan kept doggedly throwing his fastball. Some nights his pitches were wild, but they were always fast.

Nolan had received a $20,000 bonus when he signed the contract with the Mets, and he decided to use it to pay off his parents' mortgage. It was his way of saying thank-you for all they had done for him. He used the few thousand dollars he had left over to buy himself a shiny, new 1965 Chevy Impala. It was maroon with a red interior, and driving around in it increased his self-confidence.

At the end of his season in Marion, Nolan's numbers were unimpressive. He had won 3 games and lost 6. He had walked 56 batters and hit 8 with wild balls. But his manager, Peter Pavelick, saw potential in Nolan. He recommended that Nolan be one of twenty Mets players sent to Florida to play in the winter instructional league.

So Nolan reported to St. Petersburg, Florida. His new manager was tough, but the atmosphere was more positive. For the first time, Nolan had a pitching coach. He began to learn that there was more to pitching than just throwing a ball hard and fast.

When the winter league ended, Nolan went to Homestead, Florida, for minor league spring training. He knew the players who made it to the triple-A teams were only one step away from the major leagues. But he was sent to Greenville, North Caroline, a single-A team. Pete Pavelick had been moved from Marion to Greenville, so at least Nolan was working with someone familiar. Unfortunately, everything else was the same as well—long bus rides, bad fields, bad lights, bad locker rooms. Nolan was tired of the routine.

Nolan had learned a lot in the instructional league—and it showed in his game. By the end of the season, he had struck out 272 batters and won 17 out of 19 games. Nolan's best game of the season was when his parents, one of his sisters, and Ruth came down for a visit. While they watched, Nolan struck out 19 batters in seven innings.

Nolan Ryan is pictured here in his New York Mets uniform in 1968. He played with the Mets from 1966 to 1971. These years were marked by professional frustration as he was seldom included in the starting rotation.

His performance began to win the attention of newspaper reporters as well as the Mets' management. The Mets decided to call Nolan up to play with the big league team for the month of September.

During his month in New York, Nolan saw a different world. No more buses; big leaguers traveled by airplane. No more bad fields, poor lights, or cramped locker rooms, either. Nolan couldn't stay in this world yet. But he hoped, one day, he would be back.

In the meantime, the season ended. With the Vietnam War in progress, many men were expected to fulfill their obligation to the military. Nolan entered the U.S. Army Reserves in January. He completed nearly six months of training and missed spring training for baseball. But he had completed his full-time army service. He was free to return to baseball, although he would have to report to the military on many weekends.

Next, the Mets assigned Nolan to a triple-A team in Jacksonville, Florida. They wanted to give him time to develop his fastball, and Nolan was eager to learn. After he struck out eighteen batters in seven innings, his fame with the fans began to grow. When he was scheduled to start in a home game in Jacksonville, the game was sold out. But as Nolan was warming up before the game, something popped in his arm. Pain shot threw him. He couldn't pitch. Money was refunded to the crowd, and most of them went home.

Nolan spent the rest of the season working to rehabilitate his arm. The year was not a total disappointment for him, though. Ruth had graduated from high school. She and Nolan could get married at last.

But the Mets management didn't want to give him any time off. Finally, they agreed that he could get married on a Monday if he was back by Tuesday. So, on Monday, June 26, 1967, Nolan and Ruth had a big wedding celebration at the Alvin Methodist Church.

Their happy day was clouded, however, when Nolan's father got sick that morning. He was so ill that he had to be hospitalized. Nolan and Ruth left their reception and went right to the hospital. Mr. Ryan was too groggy to talk to

A family man, Nolan is pictured here with his wife, Ruth, and two of his three children, Reese *(left)* and Wendy, outside their home in Alvin, Texas, in 1979.

him, but Nolan spent time holding his hand. He knew his father was dying of lung cancer after a lifetime of smoking.

Nolan's arm slowly healed, and by the following year he was ready and eager to play. After all his stops and starts, another year in the minor leagues would have given him more time to smooth out his pitching. But the fans were eager to see him in the big league, and the Mets decided to bring him up.

Nolan started out well. He soon owned the Mets' record for the most strikeouts in a single game. But he still had to report for military duty on many weekends, and this meant he lost chances to pitch. He also had a blister on his hand that wouldn't go away. Someone suggested he soak his hand in pickle brine to toughen up his skin. He was desperate enough to try it, but it didn't work. Nothing helped.

Finally, the blister put him on the disabled list, and he missed playing for the entire month of August. To make matters worse, he was worried about his father. In July, the doctors had been forced to removed Mr. Ryan's left lung.

Nolan and Ruth were both glad when the season ended and they could go back home to Alvin. Used to small-town life, Ruth was home-sick and unhappy in the big city.

The next year wasn't any better. Nolan spent most of his time sitting in the Mets bullpen. Feeling like the forgotten man on the team, he believed that the long periods of inactivity were ruining his rhythm. He did have moments of glory—like when he helped the Mets take a 2–1

Though Nolan's years with the New York Mets were not personally productive, they did give him his only World Series ring. That was in 1969, when the "Amazing Mets" won the World Series against the Baltimore Orioles in the fifth game, shown here.

lead in the World Series they would eventually win against the Baltimore Orioles. But unfortunately, he lost more games than he won.

After the underdog Mets won the World Series in 1969, the fans went wild. The team was given a ticker-tape parade through the streets of Manhattan. Ed Sullivan asked them to appear on his national television show. Many of the players spent the off-season making as much money as they could from personal appearances. But Nolan and Ruth just wanted to get back home to Alvin. Nolan wanted to be there in time for hunting season.

With the $20,000 bonus each Mets player got for winning the World Series, Nolan and Ruth bought their first house and eight acres of land just outside Alvin. When the time came to go back to New York, they hated to leave.

Nolan began the season by pitching a near no-hitter against Philadelphia. He gave up only 1 hit and struck out 15 batters, setting a new team record. But by the end of the season, he had walked 97 batters in 132 innings. His record for the season was only 7-11.

The year's worst blow came that summer when Nolan's father finally lost his battle against lung cancer. Nolan took his father's death hard. He had relied on his father for advice, encouragement, and support. Now that his father was gone, Nolan became so discouraged that he considered dropping out of baseball altogether. Ruth convinced him not to give up yet. She believed her husband would one day achieve the success of which he dreamed.

Nolan started the 1971 season on a better note. His blister had healed, and he was back as a starting pitcher. By the end of June, he had an 8–4 record. But he fell apart in the second half of the season. When his pitching became more and more wild, he walked 116 batters. Worse yet, he wasn't enjoying baseball anymore. Something had to change.

After the 1971 season, he went to the general manager and asked to be traded. "I've been a disappointment to myself," he said. "If I didn't feel I had the potential to be a twenty-game winner, I'd quit."

Nolan Ryan needed a fresh start.

5 California Sunshine

O n November 21, 1971, Ruth and Nolan shared a wonderful event when their first son, Reid, was born. Two weeks later, Nolan was traded to the California Angels.

Eventually, the Mets realized they had made a mistake. Whitey Herzog, the team's director of player development, has said, "It might be the worst deal in history." But from Nolan's point of view, it was a wonderful deal. He and Ruth left New York and headed for sunny California.

Things didn't start out well in California, though. Reporters felt the Angels had been foolish to trade all-star Jim Fregosi for an unproven pitcher like Nolan Ryan. Meanwhile, Nolan's pitches were becoming even wilder.

The final straw came when the baseball players went on strike and no one got paid. Nolan and Ruth had a new baby to support. Nolan had to take out loans just to pay their bills. The three of them lived in a trailer home he borrowed from his sister. Once again, Nolan seriously considered quitting baseball and heading back home to Texas. And once again, Ruth convinced him to stick it out a little longer.

Tom Morgan, the Angels' pitching coach, began to spend long hours with Nolan, helping him to improve his pitch. Things finally began to fall in place for Nolan. By the end of the season, he was at the top of the American League's record with 329 strikeouts. He also led the league with 9 shutouts; his overall record was 19-16; and he had a 2.28 ERA. He finally felt as though he was where he belonged.

He and Ruth liked California, too. When he received a salary increase at the end of his first season, they were able to settle down comfortably. Nolan looked forward to the season to come.

Nolan's transfer to the California Angels in 1971 was a change he welcomed. In his first season, he pitched 284 innings, almost double that of any year with the Mets. He led the American League with 329 strikeouts and 9 shutouts and was named to the all-star team. Here he is shown securing his 300th strikeout of the 1974 season.

In the years ahead he was able to surpass even his highest hopes, pitching four no-hitters and tying Sandy Koufax's record. His pitches weren't just impossible to hit—they were too fast to even see! Batters tried instead to "hear" Nolan's pitches. "That sounded low," they would say, or, "That sounded high."

The record for baseball's fastest pitch had been set by Bob Feller in 1946 at 98.6 miles an hour. Nolan broke that record in 1974 during a game against the Chicago White Sox at Anaheim Stadium. The Angels had brought in top scientists with sophisticated electronic equipment. They used a beam of light shot over home plate from the press box to determine the speed of Nolan's pitches. They timed seven of them at over 100 miles per hour; his fastest was 100.9 miles per hour.

The 1975 season, however, brought more challenges for Nolan as well. In April, he developed a sore and swollen right elbow from loose bone chips. As the months went by, his elbow became so painful that even brushing his teeth was torture. He was also suffering from a badly pulled groin muscle. He had surgery on his elbow in late August, and his arm was in a cast until October.

With all this pain, Nolan's attitude was poor. He refused to talk to reporters, and he began to wonder if he would ever pitch again. Increased responsibilities added to his sense of being overwhelmed, as in January, he and Ruth had another son, Reese.

But as his elbow recovered, Nolan regained hope. He and Ruth had a happy family and a comfortable home in southern California. His income was climbing, and he felt a bond with the California fans. He also enjoyed the support of the Angels' owner, Gene Autry, a cowboy film star. The two had a lot in common and became good friends.

In 1977, Buzzie Bavasi was named general manager for the Angels. For some reason, Bavasi did not like Nolan. He made rude comments about Nolan to reporters, and he refused to consider Nolan's request for a salary increase, even though Nolan was making less than some other players.

Gene Autry, who parlayed playing a five-dollar mail-order guitar into a career as Hollywood's first singing cowboy, owned the California Angels during Ryan's tenure.

The contract talks became so bitter that Nolan knew he could not continue to play for Bavasi. At last, he announced that he would be leaving. Bavasi replied that replacing him would not be hard.

Nolan forgot about these tensions, though, when his daughter, Wendy, was born. And they seemed even less important when his oldest son was injured. Reid, now seven, was showing off his new Little League uniform to some other boys in the park, while his mother watched from across the street. Some of the boys threatened to rip the uniform, and Reid dashed back across the street to his mother. He never looked to see if traffic was coming. Ruth watched, horrified, as her son was struck full-on by a car.

Reid was rushed to the hospital, where the doctors took care of his broken leg. They suspected, however, that he had another, more serious injury. Ruth called Nolan immediately.

Nolan was in Boston at Fenway Park, sitting in the bullpen. Normally, players cannot be interrupted during a game, but Ruth insisted.

Once she spoke to him, Nolan changed his clothes and drove straight to the airport. When he got there, he found there was no flight until the next morning. So he spent the night in the airport, waiting, filled with anxiety.

He reached Los Angeles in time to see Reid wheeled into the operating room for exploratory surgery. The doctors discovered the boy's spleen had been damaged and had to be removed. One of his kidneys was also damaged. The doctors tried to repair it, but two weeks later, Reid was back for more surgery. This time they removed the kidney.

Reid spent the next two months in the hospital, and Ruth and Nolan took turns staying with him. Gene Autry told Nolan that his family should come first. He was allowed to skip road trips, miss starts, and not be with the team unless he was actually pitching.

Reid did recover, but after so much tension, Nolan had no heart for a bidding war over his contract. All he knew was he wanted to go home—to Texas.

Nolan Ryan tips his cap after tying legendary pitcher Sandy Koufax's record of 97 games with 10 or more strikeouts. He reached the mark in 1977 while pitching for the California Angels against the Oakland Athletics.

Back Home

In 1979, George Steinbrenner of the New York Yankees offered Nolan a million-dollar contract, but when the National League's Houston Astros matched the offer, Nolan didn't need to think twice. The Astrodome was close to his home in Alvin, and he couldn't imagine anything he'd like more than playing back in his home state. He signed a contract with the Astros that gave him a million dollars a year for three years. At the time, this was the highest-paying contract ever signed in baseball history. The people of Alvin expressed their delight with a "Welcome Back to Texas Day" in Nolan's honor.

But as happy as Nolan was to be back home, he had to make adjustments. First of all, he had been playing for the American League, and he didn't know the hitting styles of the National League players. He also had to adjust himself to the National League's strike zone. National League umpires don't call high strikes, and Nolan decided that this made the strike zone about a quarter smaller than what he was used to.

Nolan's performance during that first season was good but not great. The Astros had a serious setback that season as well, when they lost their other new pitcher, J. R. Richard. Richard had a stroke at the end of July, putting him out of the game for the rest of the season. He was never able to pitch with the same success.

By the 1981 season, however, Nolan knew the hitters he was up against, and he had gotten used to the strike zone. A two-month players' strike in June and July halted him momentarily, but when the strike was over, Nolan was ready to play.

When Nolan Ryan came to the Houston Astros in 1979 he was already a seven-time strikeout leader and had a record-tying four no-hitters. He threw his record-breaking fifth no-hitter in 1981 and led the Astros to the division title in 1980 and 1986.

Nolan pitched well. But his ERA was the lowest ever in his career, and he was finishing fewer games than before. At age thirty-four, he didn't seem to be able to pitch for more than seven innings. Twice he blew no-hitters in the seventh inning. Nolan doubted that he would ever be able to pitch another no-hitter. He was not a kid anymore.

But in September, as the Houston Astros played the Los Angeles Dodgers, Nolan got on a roll. The Astros were in the lead 3–0 as they entered the eighth inning. By the ninth inning, the score was 5–0, and Nolan was still going strong. He struck out Reggie Smith. He struck out Ken Landreaux. Then he was up against Dusty Baker, the third best hitter in the National League.

Nolan struck him out! Nolan had now thrown five no-hitters, breaking Sandy Koufax's record. The crowd went wild. His Astros teammates carried Nolan off the field on their shoulders.

That year the Astros were in the best-of-five play-offs against the Dodgers. The Astros won the first two games, but the Dodgers won the final three. Nolan was disappointed his team hadn't won, but he had still

Single Season Strikeouts			
1.	Nolan Ryan	(1973)	**383**
2.	Sandy Koufax	(1965)	**382**
3.	Nolan Ryan	(1974)	**367**
4.	Rube Wadell	(1904)	**349**
5.	Bob Feller	(1946)	**348**
6.	Nolan Ryan	(1977)	**341**
7.	Nolan Ryan	(1972)	**329**
8.	Nolan Ryan	(1976)	**327**
9.	Sam McDowell	(1965)	**325**
10.	Curt Schilling	(1997)	**319**

had a fantastic year. His record was 11–5, and his 1.69 ERA led the National League.

One reason Nolan was playing so well for the Astros was his conditioning program. Gene Coleman was the Astros' strength and conditioning coach, and he helped Nolan work out a training routine on the Astros' twenty-machine Nautilus equipment. This routine helped Nolan continue to be a strong player as he got older.

Ryan pitches strike three in the ninth inning of his fourth no-hitter. Ryan reached this milestone against the Baltimore Orioles on June 1, 1975, while playing for the California Angels.

Gene knew that a fastball's power comes not so much from the arm muscles as from the legs. Gene also wanted to concentrate on developing Nolan's stomach muscles, so there would be less stress on Nolan's arm. Baseball experts predicted that Nolan would be able to pitch for only about another three years or so, but with Gene's help, Nolan was proving them wrong. He continued to pitch and continued to break records.

For fifty-five years, Walter "the Big Train" Johnson had held the major league record for strikeouts—3,508 of them during his career between 1907 and 1927. The record had been set twenty years before Nolan was born, and everyone thought that this was one record that would stand forever.

Now, though, there were a total of four pitchers who might break that longtime record—Steve Carlton, Gaylord Perry, Tom Seaver, and Nolan Ryan. If Nolan wanted to be the one to break the record, he was going to have to hustle.

Although the Astros didn't make it to the play-offs in 1982, Nolan had a good year. He had a 16–12 record, and he finished third in the National League for strikeouts. He was now fifteen strikeouts away from Johnson's record.

But in the 1983 spring training, Nolan had some minor injuries that kept him from playing, and he even spent some time in the hospital with illness. It looked as though Gaylord Perry might break the record instead of Nolan.

Finally, in the twelfth game of the season, Nolan was able to play. Nolan got seven more strikeouts against the Montreal Expos at the Astrodome. The Astros' next game was against the Phillies, but this time Nolan pushed himself too hard. He struck out only three players, and he walked six. The Astros lost the game.

Nolan's next chance came against the Montreal Expos again. By the eighth inning, Nolan had struck out only four players—but that tied him for the record. Brad Mills was up to bat—and Nolan struck him out!

Here Texas Rangers' pitcher Nolan Ryan winds up to pitch during spring training in 1992. Talk that Nolan had begun to act more like a forty-two-year-old than a kid with a blazing fastball only made him work harder.

Even the Expos fans in the crowd were cheering. Nolan's number 3,509 strikeout had broken Johnson's fifty-six-year-old record. While the scoreboard flashed pictures of Nolan and Johnson, Nolan tipped his cap to the crowd.

Later that year, both Steve Carlton and Gaylord Perry broke Johnson's record as well, and three years later Tom Seaver smashed it,

too. These three players were at the end of
their careers, however, while Nolan was still
going strong. He decided he would aim for
4,000 strikeouts.

The next couple of seasons, however,
were disappointing for the Astros, and they
were hard for Nolan as well. A series of
injuries kept him from achieving as much as he
would have liked. By 1985, though, Nolan had
nailed strikeout number 4,000—this time the
unlucky player was Danny Heep of the New
York Mets. As his reward, Nolan was named to
his sixth all-star team. Pete Rose had set a
record of his own that year with his 4,000th
hit, and Rose and Ryan together threw out the
ceremonial first pitch.

By 1987, Nolan's arm hurt whenever he
pitched. The Astros' general manager, Dick
Wagner, decided to pull Nolan from every
game once he reached 115 pitches. He was hop-
ing to protect Nolan from more injuries. But
Nolan was frustrated. By the end of the season, he had 270 strikeouts, more than anyone
else in the league, and his ERA of 2.76 was the

league's lowest as well, but his win-loss record was 8–16 because he never had the chance to finish off a game. He was glad when Dick Wagner was fired from his position. Now Nolan's pitch limit was gone.

By the end of the 1988 season, Nolan had gone way past his original goal; he had 4,775 strikeouts! He had been with the Astros eight years, and although he had ups and downs, the years had been good ones for him. He was still earning a million dollars a year, and that was plenty for him and his family. He never asked for a raise, even though by then other players were making more than that.

But when the Astros' general manager, Bill Wood, asked Nolan to take a 20 percent cut in pay, Nolan was offended. He tried to talk to Wood about his feelings, but the Astros' manager held firm. If Nolan wanted to keep playing for the Astros, he'd have to take a cut in pay.

There were other teams, however, that were willing to pay plenty to have Nolan on their team. He wanted to stay in Texas, and the Rangers were offering him a two-year contract, with $1.6 million the first year, twice what the Astros wanted to pay him.

Nolan accepted. He would be forty-two years old going into the next season. He knew retirement was around the corner. But he had 273 wins and 4,775 strikeouts. He figured he could keep playing long enough to make it to 300 wins and 5,000 strikeouts.

He never dreamed that some of his best years of playing were still to come.

The Ryan Express

The Texas Rangers had the reputation of being one of the worst teams in major league baseball. But in 1988, the Rangers had been bought by a group of investors led by George W. Bush, son of then president George Herbert Walker Bush. George W. was determined to make his new team a winner. Promoting Nolan as the Rangers' star player was part of Bush's plan.

Above the Rangers' ticket windows now hung enormous, twenty-by-twenty-four-foot photos of Nolan pitching. The Rangers were behind Nolan 100 percent. Their support gave him a chance to begin all over again, even at the age of forty-two.

Nolan didn't let the Rangers down. He held his own against players nearly twenty years his junior. And on August 22, 1989, against the Oakland A's, Nolan reached the 5,000 mark for strikeouts. The game was stopped as the crowd erupted with applause. A video recorded earlier was played, showing President Bush congratulating Nolan on his feat.

The Rangers didn't win their division that year, but with Nolan's help they did prove that they were a team to be taken

Nolan Ryan's Strikeout Victims

Hall of Fame Hitters

Hank Aaron	4
Ernie Banks	3
Johnny Bench	7
George Brett	18
Lou Brock	8
Rod Carew	29
Roberto Clemente	6
Reggie Jackson	22
Al Kaline	3
Harmon Killebrew	11
Eddie Mathews	1
Willie McCovey	1
Joe Morgan	6
Brooks Robinson	8
Mike Schmidt	15
Willie Stargell	8
Carl Yastrzemski	7
Robin Yount	16

seriously. They showed their gratitude to Nolan by welcoming his sons to spend time with the team.

The Astros had discouraged Nolan's sons from hanging around the Dome, but now Reid and Reese Ryan, seventeen and thirteen years old, were welcomed by the Rangers as bat boys at both home and away games. They took batting practice and tossed around balls during the team practice. Pitching coach Tom House even worked with them.

Tom also worked with Nolan. He had the idea that a player could improve his performance at baseball if he also worked in another sport. Nolan was still doing the weight training he had begun with Gene Coleman at the Astros, but now he also began tossing a football to make himself a better pitcher.

Whatever he was doing seemed to be working. Five times in 1989 he had come very close to pitching another no-hitter. The fans began to wonder whether Nolan might have another no-hitter in him. They flocked to his games to see.

Nolan Ryan was still going strong with the Texas Rangers in spite of age and injuries. In this 1989 picture, Ryan, at age forty-two, prepares for a match against the Oakland Athletics.

By the beginning of the 1990 season, Nolan was suffering with constant pain, and the stress took its toll on his pitching. In May, he lost three games in a row, and then he went on the disabled list for fifteen days. When he came back, his pitching wasn't much better.

Nolan was beginning to wonder if he had reached the end of his baseball career. Ruth couldn't help but wonder the same thing. Still,

Nolan held on. In June, Ruth and two of their children, Reese and Wendy, decided to attend Nolan's game in Oakland. Reese, who was fourteen by now, suited up as bat boy. That way he could sit next to his father and massage his back.

Nolan was in a lot of pain that day. Television viewers across the country watched as Reese sensed his father's discomfort and rubbed his back again and again. Maybe the boy's fingers worked magic.

Nolan pitched four no-hit innings . . . then five . . . then seven. By then, even the Oakland crowd was cheering for Nolan. Nolan made it through the eighth inning . . . and then the ninth! He had done it! At forty-three years old, he had become the oldest baseball player to pitch a no-hitter! He had set another record as well— he was the only player with six no-hitters.

Two days later, doctors found that Nolan had a stress fracture in his back that was causing his pain. He had two choices: retire from baseball so his back would have a chance to heal, or keep pitching despite the pain.

Nolan wanted to set more records. He decided to keep pitching.

Nolan wanted his 300th win. Only nineteen pitchers had ever reached this level of achievement, including legendary players like Grover Alexander, Walter Johnson, Christy Mathewson, Warren Spahn, and Cy Young. Later that season, his determination paid off. He became the twentieth pitcher to reach the 300-win mark.

He ended the 1990 season with a 13-9 record, an amazing feat for a forty-three-year-old player. Fans across the country loved him. The "Ryan Express" seemed to be unstoppable.

But the death of Nolan's mother that same year slowed him down. She had continued to live in the same home where Nolan and his sisters and brother had grown up, and Nolan had called her on the phone every day. One day, however, she didn't answer the phone. Although there seems to have been no warning, she had died suddenly, perhaps of a heart attack. Despite his grief, Nolan knew he had made her proud.

Nolan Ryan gets a hero's ride from his Texas teammates after pitching his sixth no-hitter. Ryan, who was forty-three at the time, became the oldest player ever to pitch a no-hitter in the majors. Yet, incredibly, he had more in store for his fans.

Shutout Games

1.	Walter Johnson	110
2.	Grover Alexander	90
3.	Christy Mathewson	83
4.	Cy Young	76
5.	Eddie Plank	64
6.	Warren Spahn	63
7.	Nolan Ryan	61
8.	Tom Seaver	61
9.	Ed Walsh	58
10.	Don Sutton	58

The next year Nolan had the chance to enjoy a happier family event—he played against his own son. Reid was now a freshman pitcher at the University of Texas, and the Rangers had set up a special exhibition game with the university team. Both father and son would be the starting pitchers for their respective teams. Ruth, the pitchers' wife and mother, threw out the first ceremonial pitch. Father and son did well that season. They had a good time, and the fans loved it. Nolan Ryan had become an American hero.

But Nolan's body was wearing down. Every muscle and tendon seemed to hurt. The old scar tissue on his pitching hand tore open, and the pain in his back was a slow, constant torture. He was starting to feel old.

Nolan Ryan is carried off the field by his teammates after throwing his record-breaking seventh no-hitter in 1991 at the age of forty-four. The no-hitter came against the Toronto Blue Jays in Arlington, Texas.

In the face of all that pain, Nolan kept going. Playing against the Toronto Blue Jays, he struck out player after player. As the innings went by, the crowd became more and more excited. Across America, fans heard rumors of the game's events and went to find televisions where they could watch. In Kansas City, fans ignored the live game being played in front of them in order to watch the Rangers–Toronto game on the scoreboard. Everybody wanted to see if Nolan could make baseball history again.

And he did! Nolan pitched his seventh no-hitter. The fans gave him a standing ovation while his teammates carried him off the field on their shoulders. Ten years earlier, sports commentators had written Nolan off as a seven-inning pitcher. Now, at forty-four years old, he had shown the world what he could do.

He had had an amazing career, and he was ready for one more season. But Nolan knew it was almost time for a new phase in his life.

Unstoppable

O n September 12, 1993, the
Astrodome was packed with the
largest crowd in Texas history—
53,657 people. Three thousand of them
were Nolan's friends and family. They had
all come to say good-bye to Nolan.

Drayton McLane, the Astros' new
owner, had invited the Rangers there for
a special farewell exhibition game.
McLane knew that many Astros fans were
angry with the Astros' management for losing Nolan, and he wanted to help heal the
bitter feelings.

Sandy Koufax, Nolan's boyhood hero,
was there for the game, as were four of his
important strikeouts: Brad Mills, whose strikeout broke Walter Johnson's record; Ron

Nolan Ryan is the only player in major league baseball history to have his uniform retired by three different teams: the California Angels, the Houston Astros, and the Texas Rangers.

Two baseball legends, Sandy Koufax (*left*) and Nolan Ryan, smile during a gathering of major league baseball's all-century team in Atlanta in 1999.

LeFlore, strikeout number 2,000; Cesar Geron-imo, strikeout number 3,000; and Danny Heep, number 4,000. As Nolan was warming up before the game, he happened to notice someone else he knew in the crowd—Melba Passmore, his fifth grade teacher. Nolan went over to the stands to say hello to the eighty-one-year-old woman, and he gave her the ball he had been using. Then former president George Bush threw out the first pitch.

The 1992 season had been a hard one for Nolan. While he was recovering from knee surgery, he pulled a hip muscle—and while his hip was healing, he cut his foot. In total, he spent seventy-three days on the disabled list. When he talked things over with his wife and family, they all agreed that it was time for him to retire. After the 1993 season, he would do something new.

But he didn't have the chance to finish his last baseball season. Ten days after the big farewell event at the Astrodome, while Nolan was pitching against Seattle in the King Dome, his right elbow popped. Nolan's arm fell limp at his side, and that was it. Nolan had thrown his last pitch.

But that didn't mean Nolan was ready to stop. He had plenty of goals yet to reach. He had always wanted to spend more time ranching. He had wanted to work more with animals, and now was his chance. As he was to say later, "The type of person I am, I deal with today and prepare for tomorrow. I'm not one to reflect back on my career."

A Texas cowboy at heart, here Nolan Ryan participates in a promotion for National Western Heritage Month at the Cowboy Hall of Fame.

Nolan was happy to settle full-time with his wife Ruth on the ranch outside of Alvin. But he didn't spend his time rocking on the porch. Instead, he became a volunteer commissioner for the Texas Parks and Wildlife Board. He also took over the management of a local bank and did product endorsements for Southwest Airlines and Dairy Queen. One of his favorite projects, however, is being part owner of a double-A minor league baseball team in Round Rock, Texas. Nolan's son Reid is the team president.

In April 2000, Nolan, then fifty-three, needed heart bypass surgery. Despite all his years of exercise, he had a blockage in one of his arteries. He had begun feeling shortness of breath and a tingling in his arms at his minor league stadium. Cardiologists told him later if he hadn't gone immediately to the hospital, he might not have had a second chance.

In Arlington, Nolan's loyal fans signed a seven-foot by three-foot get-well card at the Rangers' ballpark. Everyone was amazed and shocked that someone as strong as Nolan could suffer from heart disease, but his cardiologist explained to Nolan that his condition was hereditary, rather than caused by his lifestyle. His older brother, Robert, had also had a heart attack in his fifties.

Today, Nolan has recovered from his heart surgery and is going strong. In his spare time, he fishes and hunts. But he doesn't have a lot of spare time. He owns three cattle ranches in Texas, and he owns and serves as

Nolan Ryan's Hall of Fame plaque. He was inducted in 1999.

The Number of Times Ryan Struck Out All-Star Hitters

Albert Belle	5	Roger Maris	2
Wade Boggs	6	Mark McGwire	6
Barry Bonds	3	Paul Molitor	12
Jose Canseco	8	Rafael Palmeiro	2
Will Clark	12	Kirby Puckett	8
Andre Dawson	26	Cal Ripken Jr.	4
Cecil Fielder	4	Pete Rose	13
Carlton Fisk	24	Ryne Sandberg	11
Ken Griffey Jr.	5	Deion Sanders	3
Tony Gwynn	9	Darryl Strawberry	15
Ricky Henderson	5	Frank Thomas	11
Bo Jackson	12	Mo Vaughn	2
Chuck Knoblauch	4	Dave Winfield	8
Barry Larkin	1		

How to determine batting average:
Divide the number of hits by the number of times batted, not including walks or sacrifices.

How to determine ERA (earned run average):

$$\frac{\textbf{(Number of Earned Runs x 9)}}{\textbf{(Number of Innings Pitched)}}$$

A pitcher is responsible for runs scored as a result of hits, stolen bases, putouts, bases on balls, hit batters, balks, and wild pitches.

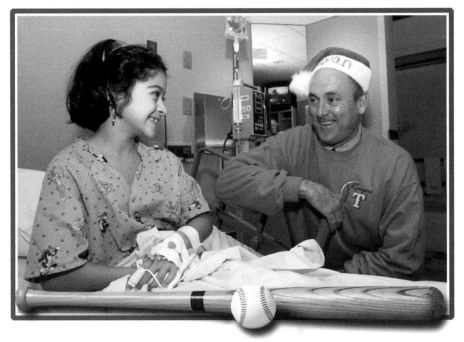

Since his retirement, Nolan Ryan has dedicated himself to several charitable causes. Here he comforts a patient, Cynthia Norris, on Christmas at the Children's Medical Center in Dallas.

chairman of the board for the Express Bank. He also owns a restaurant and a hotel. In addition, he serves on the board of directors for the Nolan Ryan Foundation, the Justin Cowboy Crisis Fund, the Texas Water Foundation, and the Natural Resources Foundation of Texas. He also hosts *Nolan Ryan Outdoors* on Fox Sports Southwest, and he has written five books: *Throwing Heat,*

Miracle Man, *Kings of the Hill*, *Pitching and Hitting*, and *The Pitcher's Bible*. Nolan may have struggled with his school work, but as he matured, he was able to accomplish a great deal.

Nolan's achievements came hard. Many times success seemed to be impossible. He could have easily given up. Instead, he kept going. And he continues to go. He is truly unstoppable.

NOLAN RYAN *TIMELINE*

	1947	Nolan Ryan is born on January 31 in Refugio, Texas; he and his family move to Alvin, Texas, six months later.
	1965	Pitches the Alvin High Yellowjackets to a state championship win. He is drafted by the New York Mets and plays for the Marion, Virginia, minor league team in the Appalachian League.
	1966	Plays for the Mets minor leagues; pitches three innings in the majors for the Mets.
	1967	Marries Ruth Holdorf.
	1968	Pitches first full season for the major league Mets.
	1969	Pitches for the Mets in the World Series.
	1971	His son Robert Reid is born on November 21; Ryan is traded to the California Angels.
	1972	Leads American League with 320 strikeouts and 9 shutouts, and is named to the all-star team.
	1973	Pitches two no-hitters; sets single-season strikeout record with 383 strikeouts.
	1974	Pitches third no-hitter.
	1975	Pitches fourth no-hitter.

⚾	1976	His son Reese is born on January 21.
⚾	1977	His daughter, Wendy, is born on March 22.
⚾	1979	Signs with the Houston Astros for $1 million a year, the first player in the history of the major leagues to earn that salary.
⚾	1983	Reaches his 3,509th strikeout, breaking Walter Johnson's record.
⚾	1985	Becomes first pitcher to record 4,000 strikeouts.
⚾	1989	Joins the Texas Rangers, has his sixth 300-strikeout season, and reaches 5,000 career strikeouts.
⚾	1990	Pitches his sixth no-hitter and wins his 300th game.
⚾	1993	Pitches his twenty-seventh and final season; retires with 5,714 strikeouts and fifty-two additional major league records.
⚾	1999	Inducted into Baseball's Hall of Fame in Cooperstown, New York.
⚾	2000	Undergoes heart surgery.
⚾	2001	Works as a farmer, rancher, banker, commercial spokesman, sportscaster, Texas Park and Wildlife commissioner, and baseball team owner.

Glossary

all-star When the best players in the American League play against the best players in the National League in what is known as the All-Star Game. The fans vote on the starting players, and team managers pick the pitchers.

American League One of the two leagues that make up major league baseball.

bullpen An area outside the playing field where the pitchers warm up.

cardiologist A doctor who specializes in treating heart diseases.

cleanup In the fourth position of the batting order; usually the team's most powerful hitter hits cleanup.

Finger Lakes A group of long, narrow lakes in central New York State.

flyball   A ball that is hit high in the air.

general manager   The person who works for the team's owners and makes the decisions about player trades and contracts.

hereditary   A trait that is passed on from generation to generation.

induction   The formal entry into an organization or society.

major league   The top two professional baseball leagues, the American League and the National League.

manager   The person who runs the team on the field. He or she wears a uniform and works for the owner and general manager.

National League   One of the two leagues that make up major league baseball.

refinery   A factory where oil is processed.

scout   A person who looks for talented young players to sign up for a team.

shutout   A game where the pitcher prevents any runs from being scored.

sidearm   A baseball pitching style where the arm is not raised above the shoulder, and the ball is thrown with a sideways sweep of the arm between the shoulder and the hip.

spleen An organ in the abdomen that filters and stores blood.

ticker-tape parade A parade given to honor important citizens; the air is filled with confetti, which was once produced by the "ticker" in a telegraph punching holes in a ribbon of paper.

World Series Major league baseball's championship played between the winners of the American League and National League play-offs.

For More Information

Legends of the Game Baseball Museum and
   Learning Center
1000 Ballpark Way
Arlington, TX 76011
(817) 273-5600

National Baseball Hall of Fame and Museum
25 Main Street
P.O. Box 590
Cooperstown, NY 13326
(888) 425-5633
Web site: http://www.baseballhalloffame.org

Nolan Ryan Foundation and Exhibit
Alvin Community College
Alvin, TX 77511
(281) 388-1134
Web site: http://www.nolanryanfoundation.org

For Further Reading

Blumenthal, Scott and Brett Hodus. *The Road to the Majors*. La Jolla, CA: Scobre, 2001.

Buckley, James Jr. *Baseball Top 11*. New York: Dorling Kindersley, 2002.

Kassof, Jerry. *Baseball Just for Kids: Skills, Strategies, and Stories*. Sydney, Australia: Grand Slam, 1996.

Lace, William W. *Sports Great Nolan Ryan*. Berkeley Hills, NJ: Enslow, 1993.

Mintzer, Richard. *The Everything Kids Baseball Book: Star Players, Great Teams, Baseball Legends, and Tips on Playing Like a Pro*. Avon, MA: Adams Media, 2001.

Reeser, Howard. *Nolan Ryan: Strikeout King*. Dublin, Ireland: Children's Press, 1993.

Roberts, Jack. *Nolan Ryan*. New York: Scholastic, 1992.

Bibliography

Anderson, Ken. *Nolan Ryan: Texas Fastball to Cooperstown.* Austin, TX: Eakin, 2000.

Bench, Johnny. *Baseball.* New York: Alpha Books, 1999.

Dickey, Roger F. *Nolan Ryan: Texas Ranger Hall of Fame Legend.* Richardson, TX: Crest, 2000.

Lace, William. *Sports Great Nolan Ryan.* Hillside, NJ: Enslow, 1993.

Murff, Red. *The Scout.* Dallas, TX: Word Publishing, 1996.

Rappoport, Ken. *Nolan Ryan: The Ryan Express.* New York: Dillon Press, 1992.

Ryan, Nolan. *Miracle Man.* Dallas, TX: Word Publishing, 1992.

Ryan, Ruth. *Covering Home: My Life with Nolan Ryan.* Dallas, TX: Word Publishing, 1995.

Index

About the Author

Ellyn Sanna, who has written more than fifty books, works as a freelance editor. She helps care for three children, a cat, a rabbit, and many other small animals.

Photo Credits

Nolan Ryan

Nolan Ryan

World Photos; p. 92 © Mark A. Duncan/AP/Wide World Photos; p. 94 © J. Pat Carter/AP/Wide World Photos; p. 98 © Michael Mulvey/AP Wide World Photos.

Series Editor

Jill Jarnow

Series Design and Layout

Geri Giordano

112